SUCCESS IS A MINDSET, NOT A THOUGHT

Michael K. Reed

Shades of Greatness, LLC

Shades of Greatness

CONTENTS

GRATITUDE

My gift to the future.

Thank you to all the people who have shaped me mentally, physically and spiritually. This book is a testament to the power of the mind. If I Can Excel, you can too!

Success is a Mindset, not a Thought

By: Michael K. Reed

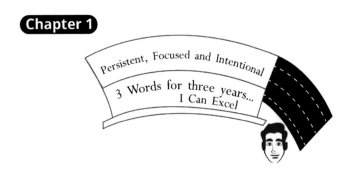

CHAPTER 1: I AM: PERSISTENT, FOCUSED AND INTENTIONAL. THREE WORDS FOR THREE YEARS, I CAN EXCEL

As I write today, Lord please allow me to do what's right. I oftentimes think about what the right thing is, but sooner than later I usually find out. I have learned that life is a journey and it's the moments in life that make each day special. Moments are defined as a short period of time. We all have moments; some we remember and others we wish we could forget. I have one special moment that inspires me to this day: the time I made straight A's in high school. It was a goal of mine for years to make all A's in a high school quarter, but I had always come short of this goal. I began to feel like it was impossible, insignificant, and simply a waste of time, but I continued to work to get all A's in high school. I don't remember the exact date, time or day but I remember the feeling of knowing that I had just accomplished a goal of mine. Moments like this motivate me to continue challenging myself. It's not the straight

A's that made this moment so special, but it's the fact that I learned if I remain persistent, focused and intentional I can achieve the goals that I set.

By being persistent, focused, and intentional I have continued to set goals. I wanted to attend college after high school. I even wanted to play on the basketball team, thought about going pro a few times but I focused my attention on attending college. To prepare for college I began to take prep courses for the ACT, an exam that some colleges used to determine if a person would be accepted into their school and if they would provide an academic scholarship. I took the ACT twice and decided enough is enough. College might not be for me. I still applied to a few colleges and universities as my high school had a requirement for graduating seniors to apply to a minimum of five colleges or universities. Upon my surprise, I began to receive acceptance letters, scholarship offers, and invites to campus tours. I decided to visit a local university to shadow a business class and heard a speech about working with people who believe what you believe and becoming a leader that people follow because they want to, not because they have to. I enjoyed this business class and was assured that I would major in business while in college. The speech was outstanding, I liked the small classroom size, and I was offered a scholarship to attend this university, but I still chose not to attend.

Fast forward a few months and I find myself at a honor society induction where the announcer says "Michael will be attending Xavier University of Louisiana and in the words of Steve Jobs, "A lot of times people don't know what they want until you show it to them." Now he would say that, right." It was at that moment that I planned to attend a university that I had not yet visited. At the time I was unsure and wondered what college life would be like. I participated in a college tour in eighth grade, but a tour is completely different from living on a college campus in a new city.

Let's think about that later. It's summertime and since my Sophomore year in high school I have had a summer internship, but this summer was different. No summer internship, just a lot of time to either prepare mentally for a new challenge or feel stuck and unsure about what was ahead of me in college. The summer of my senior year in high school I decided to set goals and for a few weeks I volunteered at a hospital. I began to realize that in order for me to accomplish the goals that I set for myself while in college I must believe that I Can Excel. I set three goals. They were to graduate college in three years, have my first play performed and get this book, "Success is a Mindset, not a Thought" published during my time in undergrad. Well, you know now the book was not published and my play "Destined for Greatness" was not performed after several calls to local theaters and no calls back. I decided to focus on graduating in three years. I was intentional in my academic journey as I always knew college was a possibility for me considering the high school that I attended for six years slogan was "College is our mission."

Yes, I attended the same high school for six years.

I began taking classes at this high school in 7th grade and continued my education at the same place for six years. It was during my high school years that I began to take college courses. At the time it was known as "dual enrollment." I was able to take college courses in high school. It was a character-building time as I balanced track practice, a school play, honor societies and various distractions that come with being the popular, high performing student that I was. Today, I can say I made it through, and it was the moments that weren't always the most enjoyable that allowed me to become a prepared leader.

I wasn't the best track sprinter, but I learned discipline and consistency from track. Each day after school there was practice and I knew that I would either be running sprints or lifting weights after a long day of classes. I would go to practice and work hard just to go out on Saturdays for a track meet and possibly not run. It was the lessons that I learned from track that allowed me to excel in other pursuits in my life. Track taught me that if I do my best, I still may not be chosen to run the race, but I know I prepared to the best of my ability.

After high school track it seemed like I was the one chosen to run the race. Not physically running, but at my Undergrad University I seemed to be the one that was often asked to participate in business competitions, do a presentation about my summer internship or take a trip to observe a new program that may be offered on campus. It did not happen overnight, but I did become a high-performing business student. After accepting to be a part of some business competition teams representing my school, I began to see some of the same personalities from high school track. It was like the same people just different names, faces and oh now they had decided to go to college and major in business like me. People wanted to win without putting the work in. To prepare for greatness it takes time, focus, persistence, and intention. A lot of times my teammates would have a good idea, great research and information but did not want to practice the presentation until the night before. During times when I was reminded of high school track and how I would put the work in and still not compete, I thought; does it make a difference if I do the right thing? Does one person really make that much of a difference? I learned, yes, I do make a difference.

It was that lesson that led me to focus my attention on the goals that I set for myself. Working to graduate in three years, after all if I wasn't performing well in my courses the university would not have asked me to represent them.

My first semester of college began, and I had six classes, one was freshman seminar. This class was once a week and provided freshman students at the university time to network and learn more about the city and university. I had my first few business courses on my schedule, but it was the Biology lecture for non-science majors that took up a lot of my time. I remember not doing well on the first quiz or exam in the course, but it was in this adversity that I became a leader academically. After I saw that this Biology lecture class was challenging my academic abilities, I created a study group with my classmates. I sent a message in a group chat informing my classmates that we could meet at the library to review for the upcoming exam and sure enough students came to review information for the test. At the end of the semester, I passed the class, but the lesson is, I am enough to make a difference and work with people who believe what you believe. The students that attended the study session believed that if we studied the material for the upcoming exam, we would do well on the exam. I finished my first semester of college with two B's and the straight A goal was still on my mind. Spring semester I came back from winter break with a goal on my mind. I secured an internship for the summer, but I knew I wanted to make all A's in college. I made all A's in high school, but college was a completely different thing. I'm preparing for my career and if I can perform at a high level now the future starts to look even brighter.

Classes began, another semester with 6 classes, more business professors and the hot, humid weather of New Orleans, LA. I remember my Accounting course that spring semester. The first day of class the teacher began by talking about signs that let you know you may need to drop his class. He was an older gentleman as I found out the year I graduated from college was his 50th anniversary of teaching at the University, but over time I learned that he had good intentions and really wanted his students to excel. I spent a lot of mornings during his office hours reviewing problems to ensure that

I understood the concepts as his exams were not multiple choice. I had to remember every step of the process and show my work.

I received my first exam back and saw a score of a 70% average. I felt disappointed after I spent so much time at the professor's office hours, practicing problems and long nights of studying. After reviewing my exam I saw that the professor marked a few answers wrong that were right, but before I met with him I took some time to think and be calm so that I would not mess up the opportunity of gaining the points that the professor had mistakenly taken away. He gracefully looked over the exam and returned it back to me during our next class. After his corrections, my grade on the exam was a high B and I felt it's not over until I win. On the remaining exams during the semester I scored A's and learned not to let what I see discourage me. At first glance I saw a C, but it was really a B that led to an A in this course at the conclusion of the semester. Not only did I have an A in this course, but in all the courses that I enrolled in that semester. I accomplished this goal twice while in college.

The second time I made all A's in college was during the spring semester of my senior year. I had 18 credit hours as I had the prior 3 semesters. During this semester I had a lot of uncertainty I wasn't sure what I would do after graduation. I was on track to graduate in three years, but I still felt that I needed to have a job upon graduation. I received a full-time offer from the company that I interned with for two summers, but

I felt that was not the best fit for me to develop my business management skills. This is a lesson: No matter what people say, follow your heart, not the crowd. Months after declining a full-time offer with a Fortune 500 company (the largest defense-contractor at the time.) I continued to apply for opportunities and receive rejections, but it was this one position that stood out to me. It was the opportunity to become a manager upon graduation. I would have the task of managing between 50-200 employees for the largest e-commerce business in the world. I accepted the offer and decided to keep it to myself. I only told my parents and continued to work that semester to become a better business leader as this was a daunting task after just being a student. I learned that I'm always a student and that's how I continue to improve.

My coursework took up some time, but I had a vision to work on my business, Shades of Greatness, LLC. I started to get a logo designed, created a mission and vision statement to guide the actions that the business would take to achieve our goal and make an impact. I made school one of my main priorities. Then a pandemic occurred "COVID-19." At first my university made classes online and the cafeteria was no longer self-serve. In about a week that all changed. Before I knew it, I was back home taking courses online, wearing a mask to the grocery store and standing six feet away from people in public. I still pressed toward the mark as I set a goal and had faith that I could achieve it. I logged in for class at the scheduled times and completed my assignments. With a few more weeks in the semester before finals I kept my goal of straight A's. The division of business had a virtual awards ceremony. I received a few awards, but the lesson is awards show my growth, not my worth.

I was proud of myself for the work I completed during my three years in college, but I knew it was a goal of mine to make straight A's once again. I waited patiently to check my grades after they were posted, I fasted and prayed during the semester for guidance and the grace to perform well in my courses. On Saturday, May 16, 2020 at 6:22pm Central Time Zone it was confirmed Michael K. Reed made straight A's once again while in college and would be graduating Summa Cum Laude, the highest honor for a college or University graduation. I shed a tear that time, but I knew there would be more tiers. I embraced the moment knowing that reels capture emotions and dreams are real. I remembered the time, date, and day this time as my grades were now online. It was special for me, but I thought the people around me would be more engaged and excited about my success.

I know I don't do things for people. I do them for myself, but the way I show support for the accomplishments people make is different. I make it known that I am proud and encourage them to keep striving towards their goals. Instead of spending time thinking about how people celebrated my success I took time to analyze the accomplishments I made throughout the past three years of undergrad. The things that I accomplished made me proud.

I began a project titled "FUND the homeless" while in high school. I donated clothing to the homeless during the winter months and spent time talking to some of the homeless people. I learned a lot from the conversations that I had with the people I donated to. One of the most profound things was that one of the men whom I spoke with was an entrepreneur before he became homeless. Entrepreneurship has been a goal of mine for a long time, but at the time I did not have my first official business Shades of Greatness, LLC.

This interaction has been a constant reminder that great power requires great responsibility and to remain humble no matter what level of success I obtain. This inspiring entrepreneur's success was distraught by him stating that he met the wrong woman and his life turned to shambles. The first FUND the homeless project was recorded and released on my social media. I hope some of the people that I spoke with are back doing the things that they love because tough times don't last, tough people do. Through the conversations that I had with those gentlemen they surely seem to be persistent, focused, and intentional. How else could the guy run a business with seven employees and the other man work at a business in downtown Chicago? It took some skill. As humans we can't believe everything we hear, but all I have is the words that people speak, and I choose to use them to uplift and not tear me down.

This FUND the homeless project continued while I was in college. I donated snacks and water to the homeless in New Orleans, LA and while spending time in Florida during the summers I was able to volunteer with Habitat for Humanity to help build a home. Years later, I started a program with Habitat for Humanity New Orleans, LA. The program was called H.O.M.E., the acronym meant Helping Others Maintain Energy. This program focused on helping the Habitat for Humanity New Orleans, LA homeowners set goals and create a plan to achieve them. I hosted one session at the New Orleans, LA Habitat for Humanity facility. This collaborative effort was altered by COVID-19 and the information became available to the homeowners through email. This is the one thing that is constant in life, change.

Some things change for the better and others may seem like they were for the worse. In those moments of uncertainty remember only God knows what's truly good. As humans we see things and say things look good but only God knows what's really good. Even when God allows good things to happen, we must know that he is the provider and praise him, not the gift. God created woman while Adam was asleep. People are still attracted to women to this day, but when Adam put Eve, the woman, before God's commandments, the woman God gave him was no longer viewed as good. No matter the challenge in life stay persistent, focused, and intentional knowing that all things work together for the good of those who love God and are called according to his purpose.

Chapter 2

Power of the mind: If I can believe it, I can achieve it!

CHAPTER 2: POWER OF THE MIND: IF I
CAN BELIEVE IT, I CAN ACHIEVE IT!

Time is divine and the future is ordained.
What's a dream without a plan? What's a journal without a pen? What's five guys without men? Dreams take
time to manifest, but when an idea comes to mind it is
important that we write it down. It may take time to
take action, but a journal and a pen is one step in the
right direction. Over time I can think about the ideas
I've had, the process I took to achieve them and the challenges I faced that made them even more real.

Let's talk about my play, "Destined for Greatness."
This play was created from a class assignment. It's
about the life of a student athlete named "Johnny Deng."
Johnny was a high school baseball player that wanted to
play college baseball and go on to play professional. His
dream did come true to play college and professional
baseball, but the play highlights the mindset of Johnny
Deng throughout the process. Every morning before

going to school or baseball practice the play highlights Johnny Deng saying a monologue. Johnny Deng's monologues went something like this, "Believe in yourself. You are a man of value. The city will love you. I am Great, Great, Great." It's the mindset of greatness that could be credited to Johnny's success. The character, Johnny Deng, teaches us that if we don't believe in our dreams and goals who will? Johnny was faced with a constant challenge of moving, seemed like every time he was comfortable and found some new friends his parents would inform him that they would be moving. The one thing that remained constant about Johnny Deng was his mindset. He knew he wanted to be great at what he did so no matter if his parents questioned his sanity for speaking to himself in the mirror, he was persistent along his journey to play professional baseball.

Not all of our dreams result in immediate success or as we planned them to happen, but trusting the process is a major part of knowing that in the due time what's for us we shall obtain. I can remember contacting theaters to have my play, "Destined for Greatness" acted out, I was persistent. I left messages, sent emails, waited patiently and still didn't receive a call back. But over time I began to trust that if God wanted my play, "Destined for Greatness" to be acted out, in his time he will make it happen. I still took steps to make sure that my work is protected when the opportunity presents itself. I got my play copyrighted and I'm still not sure what will happen with the play, but that hasn't stopped me from working to achieve other goals and ideas that come to mind.

Entrepreneurship has been a goal of mine for a while. In high school I was interested in starting a lawn care business. "Mikey's Lawn Care" was going to be the name. I did cut a few lawns, but it was not an official business. It was a taste of success, but for the lawn care business to be successful I had to believe in the idea. That was a lesson learned, people won't believe in your dreams and ideas like you do and they for sure won't put the work in for you. At the time I didn't know about creating an LLC, limited liability company, a company that protects the owner's assets from the business. "Mikey's Lawn Care" was the beginning of my entrepreneurship journey and after a summer of cutting a few lawns there was a pause.

With Mikey's Lawn Care business not running consistently, the next summer I joined an entrepreneurship program focused on presenting aspiring entrepreneurs with knowledge and the opportunity to plan, develop and present their business ideas. After long weeks of seminars with entrepreneurs speaking about their businesses, lessons learned, and services offered my group began to work on a mobile app focused on providing teens with events to attend based on their interest. We spent months creating a business plan, conducting market research, meeting with app designers, and understanding the market for our mobile app. The day to present our business idea to investors came and it was like playing hide and seek. We were a group of three, one of the group members decided to move on the day of the presentation and informed the team that she would not be able to present and the member that was there with me explained that her throat was hurting so she couldn't speak. It was all on me to present information planned to be dispersed between three people. In my mind I knew I couldn't let myself down, yes it was a team effort but at that point it was all eyes on me.

I Can Excel, If you can believe it, you can achieve it, these words pushed me past all the emotions I felt in the moment and at the conclusion of the pitch competition my group placed in the top 3. Yes, it still does make a difference if I, one person does the right thing. Just imagine if I didn't take the preparation process serious for our business, I wouldn't have been prepared to present financials, a marketing plan or research. It's the work that I did in silence that allowed me and my team to shine in public. This story confirms life continues to change, but if we believe in ourselves and put the work in great things can still happen.

Turn pain into gain:
If it's in my mind, it's in my reach

CHAPTER 3: TURN PAIN INTO GAIN: IF IT'S IN MY MIND, IT'S IN MY REACH.

As I transitioned to college I continued to be reminded of the start of my senior year of high school. The first day of school I was dressed in a salmon color polo, gray dress pants and some brown slip-on shoes. I was dressed for success as I knew after school, I had my first interview for a potential full ride scholarship to a four-year college or university. I made it to the interview safe and sound. There I was greeted by some people I knew and a room full of unknown faces as we were being watched to see how we interacted. This method of watching us was supposed to assist the committee in deciding who would be selected for the next round of interviews for the scholarship. I assume I interacted well according to their standard. Weeks later I received an email that stated I was selected for a Round 2 interview.

The day of the Round 2 interview came, and I

needed to show a graded paper at the time of my interview. It was early in the quarter and on the day of my interview I knew that I had a paper due, so I asked the professor if my paper could be graded the same day for my upcoming interview. I was excited that the teacher was able to assist me during my journey of interviewing for the scholarship. I saw the grade on the paper was a "D". I was devastated as I knew the grade was not the best reflection of my academic performance. I had no other graded paper, but that one, so I had to make it work. I made it to the interview and found out that the scholarship would not support me majoring in business at the university I was interested in. I selected another university right before my interview and explained that I could major in performing arts as I was an actor. I performed in a school play and competed in a monologue competition. I later found out I did not make it to the next round, but I did learn to perform in excellence because my current situation is the path to my next opportunity.

The path to my next opportunity was not a direct result of being denied to attend the next interview or receiving a "D" on my paper, but if I would have attended the university for performing arts I'm not sure I would be writing this book today. The scholarship interviews prepared me for my college internships with the nation's largest defense contractor, interviews for post-graduation opportunities and it allowed me time to better understand myself. Along my journey of being interviewed I have learned that taking time to self-reflect and better understand myself has allowed me to speak clearer and explain life experiences that show I am a focused, persistent and intentional person. One of the biggest takeaways is I never lose, either I win, or I learn. It's all about the mindset, delayed not denied. It's like homophones, words that sound the same but have different meanings. You can feel upset but you can also move forward and fill your mind with encouraging words that let you know if I made it past this experience there must be something better in store for me. I Can Excel.

CHAPTER 4: THE REAL ICE IS ME. OR I AM THE REAL ICE.

I know it's God's will for me to be weal. Another homophone, weal is defined as "well-being, prosperity, or happiness." In life health is wealth. Oftentimes ice is used to categorize jewelry or material possessions, but without health how can people enjoy possessions or make the money to purchase these items? I have had a lot of nicknames, but for some reason people start calling me ice, "ice man" was the name. I'm not sure if it was the way I dressed or me as a person, just one fresh young man. After long thought I turned the acronym ice into I Can Excel and that has been my brand for some time. The root to success is believing that your idea is valuable and serves a need that people have. I can remember many times while being in school or programs being asked to do an interview on how the program or scholarship impacted me.

I was needed as a source of importance, letting people who supported a program or wanted to know more about a program be ensured that the program was doing work that made a difference in the lives of others. That's why it's so important to have a mission and vision for a program or business when you are planning for success. A mission allows people to be attracted to the reason why the business or program operates, and the vision allows people to connect to the long-term goal. Your purpose guides your actions and what you do reflects your personal belief system. My business Shades of Greatness, LLC has a mission to empower, promote and support positive, brave actions that inspire others to believe they too can excel. This mission leads the business in ensuring that positive, productive, and proficient actions are highlighted in the work that we do. I'm oftentimes asked, what does your business do? There's no one answer to that because whether it's buying property, having our logo on clothing or allowing people to speak and inspire others, we are working towards our vision which is to prosper, impact and inspire people to take action towards their ideas, vision and dreams of a better life.

As humans we all have different ideas, vision, and dreams to create a better life. Shades of Greatness, LLC is a physical representation of some of my ideas, vision, and dreams. If I Can Excel, you can too! If I put the work and time in to create an impactful book, purchase property and run a business, all ideas, dreams and vision of mine, you can too. Take the time to work towards your goals. What makes us all unique is that out of the billions of people in the world's population there's only one of each of us. There's only one Michael K. Reed. An interesting thing to me is how a teacher can assign a paper to a classroom full of students to write about a topic and no one writes the same exact paper. People may mention the same information but there will be something different about each paper. That's what makes each person unique. Lesson learned, be you, do you, for you. Remember, you are the real ICE.

Graduated from the past : I'm enjoying my present

CHAPTER 5: GRADUATED FROM THE PAST: I'M ENJOYING MY PRESENT.

Life is a gift so we must use it wisely, taking time to enjoy the present and taking steps to create a better future. Success is one the biggest prohibitors to more success. People become comfortable in their past success and sometimes stop working towards the other goals that they have in life. Life is a set time; it differs for each person, but we must make an impact with the time that we do have.

"Michael Kelly Reed Jr. Summa Cum Laude, Honors in business." The announcer said my name right, but during my virtual graduation my last name was spelled with a K. "Keed" was how it was listed alongside a photo of me with one of my most impactful awards while in college. The award from the photo was a result of working with a purpose. Me and a group of students spent a semester working with a non-profit organization to create a business incubator that would assist entrepreneurs in their journey to creating a successful business. We presented our plan of an incubator for funding. We received funding and a glass award. I did well in other competitions, but this one felt good considering it was to assist an organization focused on improving the community.

Back to this mistake, graduation is online, and my name is not spelled right. I sent the link to so many people anticipating that my name would appear as Michael K. Reed. All in all, a mistake was made, and it is now being talked about in my book. This mistake was small considering the joy I had knowing that I would not have to sit for as long as I would have if the ceremony was in person. My major concern was my diploma. I thought as long as my diploma had my name spelled right, I'm good. Graduation is over I'm relaxing receiving encouraging text and calls then I hear something about people coming over. I was not a big fan of celebrations, I was always thinking what's next, and plus it was quarantine people are supposed to be home.

I was about to leave and get some fresh air, the family asked me to stay for a few minutes as some people were coming over, just to give me cards. I was told to put on my cap and gown again to take more photos outside. To my surprise there was a row of cars and loud horns as people were handing me cards and saying their congratulations. I had a face mask on and was smiling ear to ear. I began to give the people food and kept my distance. This moment will be a memory for years to come as a drive thru graduation celebration is epic. I was upset at first about the idea of people coming over, but I stayed around and experienced laughter, memories, and happiness. I apologized so many times for my attitude about the idea of having people come over because after all it was a great success.

In life as people we experience fear, uncertainty and don't always have a clear direction on what way we should go, but it is important that we try new things and continue to work to improve ourselves. In this present moment I am writing and constantly meditating in preparation for my role as a manager of 50 plus people. I know I have training before I assume the role, but there's only so much school can teach. To get things accomplished you have to take steps in the right direction and continue to learn as you go. My name was spelled wrong on the screen, but my diploma had my name spelled correct and I know for sure it was me that graduated in three years, Summa Cum Laude and with Honors in business. It's important to focus on the things that really matter. In life we must do things that make a difference. Not for recognition, but for pure intention. My graduation is an inspiration to others letting them know if you put your mind to it, it's possible. Lesson learned, my accomplishments are bigger than me and I must continue to achieve my goals to make sure that Shades of Greatness, LLC mission and vision are accomplished.

Time is divine : Lesson Learned

CHAPTER 6: TIME IS DIVINE: LESSON LEARNED

The future is ordained, means it is already set. This does not mean that a person should not strive to improve or seek opportunities that bring the best out of them. What it means is that there is no need to stress or worry as you can only control the controllable. In life a person can control themselves and make sure that they do what they can to accomplish their goals and plans in life. There is a major distinction between easy and simple.

Setting goals is a major part of the process when working to achieve a better life or outcome for yourself. If a person has a goal to lose weight it's simple to say, I'm going to work out five times a week, eat at least one salad a day and drink 3 cups of water. When the time comes to work out and change your eating habits, is it easy? It takes time, to create habits and to break them. It takes times to build confidence after hearing more No's than you hear Yes. When you know time is divine you have a sense of ease as you work towards your goals in life. You must know that in due time I will obtain what is for me.

Lesson learned: hard and impossible are two different things. Make it happen. I remember my first summer of college having to move for an internship. It was difficult to transition from going to school in the same city that I lived in for years and then starting to intern in a new city was another challenge. I overcame the challenge and received high ratings on my performance evaluations. The key to this success was patience and consistency. At the beginning of my internship I was told the task that they wanted me to assist with, I knew it was an important project because the departments audit results determined if they could continue to operate. I took the approach of watching other employees' complete tasks as I took notes and studied the process to effectively do my part when the time came. After I was proficient in one thing, I continued to work with new people to understand other areas of the business. I repeated the same process of taking notes to understand a new process. My consistency and willingness to learn allowed me to interact with new people and make an impact on the entire team. Patience is what allowed me to understand that there was no need to rush to start doing the task, but in due time when I was proficient at the task I would then be able to assist by using the skills that I obtained.

Imagine if I started doing the work without taking time to study the process. I'm not sure that I would have been able to make a positive impact on the team. Another time when I developed my skills before taking on a new project was when I joined the intern volunteer committee. My task was to assist with creating opportunities for other interns to volunteer in the local community. I was prepared for this opportunity as I had previously started my own community service project and gained experience in budgeting, planning, and working with others to accomplish a goal. As a team we were able to plan a food drive and beach clean-up. These were two successful projects as they made an impact on the communities that we planned to serve.

Upon joining the intern volunteer community, I felt that it was important to create a mission statement that would guide the actions that we should take. Since we were interns at an organization that had a mission statement explaining that they put their customers first, I created a mission statement that read, "The mission that leads to service!" I was very creative during the process of planning for the community service events. The food drive event was named "Heal the Ache" referring to the statistic "1 in 6 American children may not know where their next meal is coming from." The goal of the food drive was to collect canned goods and funds that could be used to purchase more non-perishable items to assist the children and families in need. As I had experience with planning projects, I knew that with great power comes great responsibility. When the time came to collect the funds for the food drive, I made it clear that members of the committee should purchase the items and not just make a cash donation to the food bank organization. It wasn't that I didn't trust the organization, but I knew that it was important to ensure that our original goal of feeding the children and families was accomplished.

As mentioned before, you can only control the controllable. I made sure that my opinion on the issue was heard, but as we know opinions are like heads, everybody has one. Other members disagreed, and they won. The cash was donated directly to the food bank along with the collected items. In a collaborative effort like this I had to trust that the people on the committee had good intentions just like mine and hoped that the people in need would be fed. After all, we all won because we made a difference in the lives of others. I learned that there is more than one way to get a goal accomplished.

There are many ways to write a story or even count to ten. If I say I went to college for three years, then I started working for one of the largest e-commerce businesses in the world, a person may think that I didn't receive my diploma after those three years. If I wrote the story like this; College was a journey. In three years, I met new people, traveled the world, and learned to stay true to myself, people may think that college allowed me to gain some new experiences, but I guess he couldn't stay for the last year. The point is it's all about how we write the story and in life you have complete control of how your story is read. We can't control everything that happens in life, but we can control how we respond.

As I continue to write I, Michael Reed spent three years in college sharpening my gift, God-given talents and built more confidence to take action. College was cool, lots of time to have fun but I knew my purpose was bigger than this moment. I took action, took six classes for six semesters, went to college for three years and left with a degree. Many people start things, but it's nothing like finishing what you started. If I Can Excel, you can too! Start today and decide how your story will be read.

CHAPTER 7: BE GREAT AND GRATEFUL

Woke up this morning, that's great. Had food on the table, a place to sleep last night and I know God is able, I'm grateful! Make it all count. Moments don't last forever, but memories do. I can remember taking trips to see my Great Grandmother and she would make biscuits that the family loved. We may have taken her cooking for granted because those moments became history and before our eyes, times changed. Things will change, some for the better and others not so much but it's the lessons that are learned from those experiences that make each moment special.

Memory is one thing that should not be taken for granted. In my play "Destined for Greatness" Johnny Deng's mother began to repeat some words and forget things that she would normally remember. Johnny Deng's mother Tina was not diagnosed with a memory loss disease in the play, but she is an example of why we must be grateful for all the things that we have. In life we sometimes become so focused on working to achieve our goals and dreams that we don't take time to embrace what we do have. Instinct, Clarity and Excellence. The instinct to do the right thing, clarity to make informed decisions that will impact our future and the excellence to perform to the best of our ability every chance that we get.

These are all characteristics controlled by the mind. We must consciously take time to enjoy the life we have. I think back to a time when I wanted a lot of different gym shoes. I had shoes, but I wanted more and at that time the shoe brand that I wanted would constantly sell out. I had to learn that no matter how many shoes I had I could only wear one pair at a time, and not only that, the money I saved could be used to invest in my personal dreams that result in me having true pleasure. I began to focus my attention on my personal goals and realized with material things when you have the resources to purchase them, if they are available, they can be purchased. It's the things in life that have to be created that take some time but result in true satisfaction.

We all have ideas that come to mind, but very few of us take the time to plan for success. In a study that was completed it was confirmed that people with written goals are more likely to be successful. How much time do you spend planning for your million-dollar idea? It takes time, faith and opportunity for ideas, dreams, and vision to come to past. Approach every opportunity with your best effort. You don't know what's next and it's practice for your future opportunities.

One man complained about the color of his shoes until he met a man with no feet. Lesson learned: Take the time to be great at what you do but be grateful for what you have. We are creatures of habits, but who's going to teach us to live lavish? The mind is gold and positivity is what we need. Keep the faith, even the tallest tree started with a seed.

Create the atmosphere : Create the scene

CAUTION : I CAN EXCEL CAUTION : I CAN EXCEL

CHAPTER 8: CREATE THE ATMOSPHERE: CREATE THE SCENE

We have seen many things happen in history, but it's up to us to create the scene. Don't dwell on the past create the future. There's nothing new under the sun, but I still find a way to shine. It is important that a person focus on the power that they do possess. The power to control their mind and focus their attention on things that can change the future. There is power in our mind and the words that we speak can manifest. Choose your words wisely, what you say can become and what you do is already done.

Smiling as I stride, tomorrow is not promised, but today is considered a victory. Take life one moment at a time, one day at a time, one step at a time. Control each moment by creating a feeling of importance, knowing that you make a difference. It's the belief in yourself that allows you the confidence to pursue your goals and aspirations. Take time to write self-affirmations letting yourself know that you are capable of becoming the person that is able to achieve the goals that you have set for yourself.

Create atmospheres where you feel inspired, motivated and take action. Pinning my thoughts to paper writing history. Walking through the darkest of valleys, exploring life as I solve mysteries. It's the shortest month of the year, but everyday is a chance to make history!

Don't confuse Success with Support

It only took time...

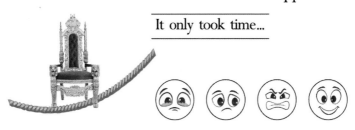

CHAPTER 9: DON'T CONFUSE SUCCESS WITH SUPPORT

Success is a result of putting the work in and good fortune, but it comes with a lot more than a person could plan sometimes. In the process of setting goals there will be people who don't believe in your dream, but when you accomplish what you had in your mind their expressions may change. There are many definitions of success, but in some things success is defined. When a person starts a project, the goal is to finish the project. The project is considered a success when it is complete. Each person may have different metrics on how they measure the success of their individual performance during the project, but the project is complete.

When I say success is defined differently for each person, I'm referring to those things that you are passionate about, that make you smile when you wake in the morning: the thought of writing a book, graduating college, making a difference in the world, or finishing something that you have been working on or procrastinating about. What I've learned is that success and support are not one in the same, and when you become successful people begin to congratulate you and take the role that they believed in you all along. People show support in different ways, but it doesn't take someone telling me that what I'm saying is not possible but when the goal is accomplished, they say my timing was impeccable to realize that success and support are not the same thing.

Even if a person doesn't agree with the approach that you take to reach a goal there are common tips that can be beneficial throughout your journey. Pay attention to the atmosphere that you have created and keep people around you that motivate you. People don't always have to agree with what you say or your plan to obtain something but know the true intentions of the people that are around you. Be cautious with who you tell your dreams, ideas and vision to, there are few people that will embrace you and truly have the means to assist. Know the difference between the assets and liabilities in your life. Assets are things that provide value to you and liabilities are things that can take away from you. Most things that you hear are not as good as they sound.

For example, a young man named Kelly from Chicago, Illinois, he grew up in the windy city believing that his dreams were possible. He always knew he wanted to be in business, so he started a business, went to college, and majored in business management. He met people along the way who said major in accounting, you'll always have a job. Become a doctor or dentist, you want some guarantees in life. He felt alone and unsure, but he stuck with his plan. He knew it was possible, that if he became valuable in business he could make as much or even more than a doctor. Through his journey he was intentional and accepted opportunities that would help him accomplish his goals and make a difference.

Do you call the people along the way that were not supporting Kelly's goals distractions or are they just a part of the process testing Kelly's true desires and passions? In life there are many tests and changes but when you know why you do something, it's hard to stop no matter the challenges that may occur. Kelly became a successful entrepreneur and I'm sure some of the same people that said he should be an accountant, dentist or doctor were or would be smiling asking Kelly how he did it.

Focus allows a person to keep going no matter what the people around them may say or do. Control the controllable take it one step at a time and know what's for you, you shall have in due time. Don't take the first step, take the right step. There will always be opportunities that look good but take some time to weigh the pros and cons of a decision. How will this impact me in the future, and will it make me a more valuable person? It's not just about you all the time. The more resources a person has the better equipped they become to assist others. There are more people in poverty than there are billionaires in the world, this proves that just because you have more people doesn't mean you can always do more.

It's important to take time and build trust with the right people. Understanding how relationships are formed is important. If you meet a person and you all become connected from complaining about the way a business operates, the future of the relationship could either be continuous complaining or actions that cause change within the business operations. Control your mindset and keep your conversations positive. What better way to compliment a person than to tell someone else something good about them? Believe in your goals, dreams and vision letting people know that If I Can Excel, you can too!

It's already done.

CHAPTER 10: IT'S ALREADY DONE

Don't stop when you're tired, stop when you're done. Success is a Mindset, not a Thought. I'm a writer and I barely want to read what is wrote. I wasn't the first one to read, but I always was the first one to dream. I had ideas on ways to make things change for the better, but I hardly ever was active in making the change I thought of.

The key to my locked mind was success, I had the thought many times to be successful but at the beginning of the day success is not a thought, it is a mindset. There are steps to get in this mindset. First you have to dream. When you dream you have the options of a dream coming true or just being stuck in the dream. Now that you have dreamed, it's time to take steps to make this dream a reality. You have to compare and contrast your dream with realities. You have to say; this is my dream, but a plan is needed to make it reality.

Think about life today. Set goals in the morning and accept rewards in the evening. This is said to mean work towards something now and live with everything forever. When you go out into your field you must put forth all the effort needed to accomplish a goal. Think often and work smart, don't overthink but have morals and rules to follow while you are in your field.

Don't let family be a distraction in your success because when you classify family it is a deep connection with people you have been around for some time and have the same blood, but what can you do with this blood in the end?

There are all different types of blood and people so watch the haters, motivators and experimenters. Some may motivate you hoping for you to fail and some may be experimenting with your feelings and dreams. When you receive help and compliments just accept and live with them, always keep them on the side of your mind because even when negative people start to talk, turn negative into positive and turn positive into success. Knowing that what's for me I shall have and remain blessed.

Made in the USA
Monee, IL
12 November 2023